# MARY-KATE & ASHLEY'S
# Walt Disney World
# ADVENTURE

by Nancy Krulik

Disney
PRESS

New York

A PARACHUTE PRESS BOOK

*The publisher wishes to thank*
*David Roark, Mark Drennen, Mark Ashman, Judy Katschke, and Hubert Kennedy*
*for their invaluable help in creating this book.*

A PARACHUTE PRESS BOOK

For information address Disney Press, 114 Fifth Avenue, New York, New York 10011-5690.
First Edition
1 3 5 7 9 10 8 6 4 2
This book is set in 15-point Garamond.
Designed by Kristina Albertson
Library of Congress Cataloging in Publication Card Number: 98-84798
ISBN: 0-7868-3205-3

For more Disney Press fun, visit www.DisneyBooks.com

# MARY-KATE & ASHLEY'S
## Walt Disney World
# ADVENTURE

"What should we do today, Ashley?" Mary-Kate asked me.

Before I could answer, the mailman arrived with a large box. "Special delivery for Mary-Kate and Ashley Olsen," he announced.

"Cool!" Mary-Kate cried. "Who's it from?"

I glanced at the address label. "It doesn't say," I replied. "But there's one way to find out!"

We quickly tore open the box and peered inside.

"Hey, look at these!" Mary-Kate pulled two pairs of Mickey Mouse ears from the box.

"And look!" I shouted. I held up a colorful map. "A map of Walt Disney World—in Florida!"

Mary-Kate jumped up. "Ashley! Two tickets to Disney World! For *us*!"

"Awesome!" I cheered.

"Where did all this come from?" Mary-Kate asked.

"Who knows?" I replied. "Who cares? We're going to Walt Disney World!"

"Are we really here at Walt Disney World?" Mary-Kate cried as we entered the park. "Or am I dreaming?"

"We're really here," I replied. "Should I pinch you to prove it?" I gave Mary-Kate's arm a gentle pinch.

Mary-Kate yanked her arm away, laughing. Suddenly her eyes locked on something behind me. "Ashley, look!" She pointed to a building the shape of a huge silver ball. "What's that?" she asked.

"That's Spaceship Earth, the symbol of EPCOT," I told her. "EPCOT is where our adventure begins."

"What is EPCOT?" Mary-Kate asked.

"EPCOT is one of four parks at Walt Disney World," I explained. "The other parks are Magic Kingdom, Disney-MGM Studios, and Animal Kingdom."

"Um, I knew that," Mary-Kate said unconvincingly.

"EPCOT has two parts—the World Showcase and Future World," I continued.

"Ashley, how do you know all this?" Mary-Kate peered at me suspiciously. "We've never been here before."

"I'm just very smart," I told her as I flipped the hair off my shoulder. "And it also helps to have the map!" I pulled the map from behind my back. We looked at it together.

Mary-Kate smiled. "Let's go!"

"This is like a dream come true," I said as we wandered through EPCOT.

"Did someone say *dream*?" a voice behind us asked.

We spun around and saw a man with a long beard and a big top hat. He held a small purple dragon with orange horns.

"I'm Dreamfinder, and this is Figment," the man said. "Welcome to Walt Disney World, the place where all your dreams can come true!"

Dreamfinder handed Mary-Kate a piece of Mickey Mouse-shaped paper.

It said:

WHO SENT YOU HERE?
TIME WILL TELL.
A GENIE? FAIRY GODMOTHER?
TINKER BELL?
ONE THING IS TRUE
AND SURE TO BE—
YOUR NEXT CLUE
AWAITS YOU IN THE SEA.
P.S. KEEP ALL YOUR CLUES.
THE WORDS IN RED WILL ADD UP TO
A VERY SPECIAL SURPRISE!

Whoa! What did the note mean? I was about to ask Dreamfinder, but when we looked up, he and Figment had vanished.

"Wow!" I cried. "Mary-Kate, what do you think is going on here?"

But Mary-Kate was concentrating on something else. "Ashley, turn around—quick!" she exclaimed.

I spun around. I didn't see anything. "What is it?" I asked.

Suddenly I was hit in the face by a stream of cold water.

We both laughed. Streams of water leaped from hidden fountains all around us. You never knew where the next spurt was coming from—or where it was going.

"No wonder they call this Leapfrog Fountains," I said, reading the map. Suddenly I got a great idea. "I bet I can get wetter than you can," I challenged my sister.

"You're on!" she replied.

After we played in Leapfrog Fountains, Mary-Kate wanted to look for our next clue.

"Our note says we'll find it in 'the sea,'" she said.

"The sea?" I repeated. "There's no *sea* in Walt Disney World."

"Hey, there's a sign that says 'The Land'!" Mary-Kate pointed toward a huge glass building. "Maybe the sea is near The Land!"

She took off for the big front doors of The Land. I caught up with her inside.

"Whoa! This is the most amazing greenhouse I've ever seen!" Mary-Kate exclaimed.

"All the vegetables, fruits, and plants are giant-sized!" I cried.

We waded through a patch of bright yellow sunflowers that were taller than we were. "These flowers are the size of trees," I said, amazed.

Mary-Kate picked up a yellow squash that was as long as her arm. She held it like a baseball bat. "Batter up!" she joked.

I grabbed several huge lemons. They were *heavy*! "Imagine how much lemonade we could make with these, Mary-Kate!"

"I don't think the sea's around here, Ashley," Mary-Kate said as we left The Land. "See if the map says anything."

I studied the map. "Well, here's a place called the Living Seas—" I began.

"That has to be it," Mary-Kate decided. "Let's go!" She took off running to the Living Seas.

"This place is huge," I said when we stepped in front of a giant aquarium. "It's like a giant glass bubble under the ocean!"

"And I've never seen so many different kinds of fish," Mary-Kate remarked.

We watched as brightly colored saltwater fish darted around happily. Dolphins and sea lions played a game of chase. Sea turtles, parrot fish, and stingrays glided through the water. Mean-looking sharks and barracudas glared at us through the glass wall.

"Yikes!" Mary-Kate said with a shiver. "I hope our clue is hidden on *this* side of the glass."

"Mary-Kate, do you see what I see?" I pointed at the glass wall that separated us from the fish.

"It looks like . . . a person!" she cried.

We leaned closer to the glass. "There's a scuba diver in there!" I exclaimed.

The diver waved in our direction. I looked around. No one stood behind us. "Is he waving at us?" I asked.

The diver held a piece of paper up against the glass. It was on Mickey Mouse–shaped notepaper. It was another note!

"Ashley, that's our clue!" Mary-Kate said excitedly.

"Quick! We have to write this down!" I pulled a pen and some paper from my pocket and wrote:

5-5-5-4-7-6-2
DIAL IT QUICK FOR
YOUR NEXT CLUE.
THE VOICE YOU HEAR
WILL TELL YOU ALL
SO HURRY OFF
AND HAVE A BALL.

"This is one amazing adventure," Mary-Kate said as we wandered through EPCOT.

"And one amazing place," I added. "So let's find a phone to see what's next."

We left the Living Seas to look for a phone.

"Hey, look at the old-fashioned cottages!" Mary-Kate pointed. "And the pretty flower gardens."

"We must be at the World Showcase," I told my sister. "This is where we can see what other countries around the world are like. I guess we've just arrived in England."

"Right you are," Mary-Kate said in a pretend British accent. "Hey, there's a phone!" She pointed to a bright-red phone booth. "The note said to call that number for our next clue. Let's go!"

We squeezed into the phone booth together. I quickly dialed the number.

"Hullo?" a voice said.

"Who's this?" I asked.

"Yuck, yuck, yuck," the voice replied.

I'd know that voice anywhere. "Goofy? Is that you?"

"Yup," Goofy answered. "Now listen carefully. I have a very important message for you."

Mary-Kate and I pressed our ears to the receiver. Mary-Kate wrote the message down on a piece of paper:

IN MEXICO
YOU TWO WILL MEET
A QUACKY FRIEND
WITH BIG WEBBED FEET.
YOU'LL FIND HIM UNDER
THE BRIGHT BLUE SKY
NOT IN A CASTLE
WITH A TOWER HIGH

"Mexico, here we come!" Mary-Kate cheered as we hurried out of the phone booth.

We stopped in front of a long row of buildings of all different shapes and colors.

"Where are we?" Mary-Kate asked.

I looked at our map. "That's France, Germany, Morocco, Japan, China, Italy. Hey, let's do a little sight-seeing before we head to Mexico."

"What about our next cl—?" Mary-Kate broke off suddenly. She stared into the distance. "Ashley, isn't that our friend Jill?" She pointed toward a crowd of people.

I shook my head. "It can't be," I replied. "Jill's at her grandma's this weekend."

But Mary-Kate was already running toward the crowd. "Let's catch up with her!" she shouted over her shoulder.

I chased Mary-Kate all the way to France.

I saw the Eiffel Tower, a colorful flower market, and a sweet-smelling perfume shop. But no Jill.

"Mary-Kate, I'm sure it wasn't Jill," I told my sister when I finally caught up to her.

"Yeah, you're probably right," she replied.

Mary-Kate spotted a cart filled with all kinds of souvenirs. "Ashley, come see this."

I picked up a little Eiffel Tower statue from the cart. "I could climb *this* tower—no problem," I joked.

Then Mary-Kate's eyes lit up. "Gargoyles!" she cried. She held up a little gargoyle figurine. "That's a scary face."

"Not as scary as this." I rolled my eyes up into my head and stretched my mouth into a weird shape.

"Okay, you win," she told me, laughing.

Mary-Kate grabbed my hand. "Come on," she said. "Let's go to Mexico for out next clue."

"Hey, look at this cool marketplace!" Mary-Kate said when we got to Mexico. Stalls were piled high with all kinds of Mexican crafts, hats, and colorful blankets.

Mary-Kate grabbed a huge blue hat from a market stall and clapped it on my head. The hat covered my eyes.

"Hey! Who turned out the lights!" I cried.

I picked up a big red hat and plopped it on Mary-Kate's head. We had a great time trying on the *sombreros*. But the fun in Mexico was just beginning. . . .

"Hey, there's Donald Duck!" Mary-Kate cried. "I bet he's the 'quacky friend' from our last clue!"

"Hi, Donald!" we both called. Donald gave us big hugs.

Then he handed us another note:

AT DISNEY-MGM STUDIOS YOU WILL FIND A MAN WHO'S STRONG AND VERY KIND. HE'LL BE YOUR COACH AND CARRY YOU ALL THE WAY TO YOUR NEXT BIG CLUE.

Donald waved good-bye and waddled off.

"Bye, Donald," we said together.

I read our clue again. "Remember, our first note said that the words in red were special? What do you think 'coach' means in this note?"

Mary-Kate shook her head. "I don't know. But I guess we'll find out." She pulled me by the hand. "Come on, Ashley. Let's go to Disney-MGM Studios for our next clue!"

"Hooray for Hollywood!" I sang as we entered the gates of the Disney-MGM Studios.

Suddenly the strongest man I'd ever seen picked up Mary-Kate and me.

"It's Hercules!" Mary-Kate exclaimed. "My hero!"

Hercules carried us all the way down Hollywood Boulevard.

"This is the only way to travel," I said.

Then Hercules gently placed Mary-Kate and me back on the ground. "Want to meet some of my friends?" he asked.

"Sure!" Mary-Kate and I replied together.

Who could they be?

"Hello, Mary-Kate and Ashley!" a voice called out.

We turned to see Buzz Lightyear and Woody from *Toy Story* coming our way. Right behind them were Aladdin and Jasmine from the movie *Aladdin*!

"We come in peace," Buzz announced.

"And with a message," Aladdin added. He handed us another note.

Buzz, Woody, Aladdin, Jasmine, and Hercules waved good-bye as we headed off in search of a "frightening show."

AT A FRIGHTENING SHOW
YOU'RE SURE TO VIEW
SOME SCARY GUYS,
BOTH OLD AND NEW.
A CLUE AWAITS,
SO DON'T THINK TWICE
JUST SCAMPER THERE
LIKE LITTLE MICE.

I turned to Mary-Kate. "They knew our names! And everyone else seems to know us, too! How come?"

"I don't know," she replied. "But I bet it has something to do with the big surprise at the end of our adventure."

I read our new clue again. "What do you think this one means?" I asked my sister.

But Mary-Kate had vanished again. I finally found her in a store down the street buying two pairs of sunglasses.

"If we're going to be in Hollywood," she explained, "we should look like movie stars."

"Hey, Mary-Kate," I said as I slipped on my shades. "There's that famous Chinese theater." I pointed to a red and gold building that looked like a Chinese palace. "That's where movie stars leave their handprints and footprints in the cement. Let's go see!"

Mary-Kate and I squatted down and placed our own hands over handprints made by Robin Williams, Michael Jackson, Christie Brinkley, and Tom Cruise.

"Wow!" I said. "I can't believe so many famous people were here!"

As we compared our hands to the handprints in the cement, two older girls walked by.

"That Tower of Terror ride is the coolest," one girl said.

"Yeah," the other one replied. "It's the *scariest* ride I've ever been on."

I looked at my sister. "Did she say *scary*?"

Mary-Kate's eyes lit up. "Maybe Tower of Terror could be the 'frightening show' from the note!"

"Could be," I replied. "Let's go find out!"

The Twilight Zone Tower of Terror looked like an old, run-down hotel. It was thirteen stories high.

"The map says this is the tallest attraction in Walt Disney World," I said as we entered the hotel lobby.

"And the spookiest, I bet," Mary-Kate said.

A creepy-looking bellboy explained to us that the hotel was struck by lightning many years ago. Now ghosts wander the halls.

"Going . . . up?" a spooky voice asked as the elevator doors creaked open. We stepped in and strapped ourselves into our seats.

"It's really dark in here," I whispered to Mary-Kate as the doors slid shut.

I couldn't see my sister, but I knew she was there. That's because she was grasping my arm—hard!

Suddenly I heard a screech. The elevator jerked upward and started racing to the top of the tower.

When we reached the top, the elevator came to a sudden stop. Then we flew down the elevator shaft at a million miles an hour!

"AAAAAAAHHHHHHHHHH!!!!!!"
we screamed.

"Boy, that sure was scary!"
Mary-Kate cried as we left the
elevator.

"Totally!" I agreed. "I'm
shaking all over."

"Want to do it again?" she
asked.

"You bet!" I said.

We went up and down in that
scary elevator three more times!

When we came out we bought T-shirts that
said I SURVIVED THE TOWER OF TERROR.
We high-fived. Awesome ride!

"Well, there was no clue there," I said as we walked away from the Tower of Terror. "But now I have serious goosebumps."

"Did you say *Goosebumps*?" Mary-Kate asked. She pointed to a sign that read GOOSEBUMPS FRIGHT SHOW. "Get ready for some more. I think we're about to get our next clue."

"I never knew magic shows could be so scary!" I told my sister after the show. "The evil rabbit was my favorite part."

"Talk about a bad hare day!" Mary-Kate joked.

"So where's our clue?" I asked.

Just then we bumped into Slappy, a life-sized ventriloquist's dummy. This dummy had a voice of his own—and a bad attitude. He was with Prince Kho-Ru, a really evil-looking mummy. His bandages were old and tattered.

"Pee-ew!" Mary-Kate whispered. She held her nose. "That's one stinky dude."

The mummy handed us a note. It read:

DO NOT SEARCH FOR YOUR NEXT CLUE— SOMEONE SPECIAL WILL FIND YOU. A CHARMING PRINCE WHO'S LOTS OF FUN AT WALT DISNEY WORLD HE'S NUMBER ONE.

"That's the hardest clue so far," Mary-Kate said as we strolled through Disney-MGM Studios. "Someone will find us? But how do we know where?"

"I don't know," I answered. "I guess we'll find out!"

"Mary-Kate, take a look at that playground over there," I said.

"Wow!" she gasped. "Everything is enormous. No, it's bigger than enormous—it's humongous!"

Blades of grass towered over us. A spiderweb was wide enough to catch our whole family. A leaky garden hose was big enough to crawl through.

"Ashley!" Mary-Kate looked at me with big eyes. "I think we just got shrunk!"

"No," I replied. "I think we just found the *Honey, I Shrunk the Kids* Movie Set Adventure."

"I feel like I'm the size of an ant," Mary-Kate said.

"Speaking of ants, check out that big one over there!" I told her. "He must be ten feet tall!"

"Come on," Mary-Kate urged. "This may be our one and only chance to ride on the back of an ant. Let's do it!"

We climbed on the giant ant. "You can see everything from up here!" Mary-Kate said. "Hey, Ashley, look over there!" she cried, pointing. "There's our friend Sarah!"

Before I could say a word, Mary-Kate jumped off the ant and ran toward the girl. She tapped the girl on the shoulder. "Hey, Sarah, what are you—" she started to say.

The girl turned around. It wasn't Sarah!

"Ooops! Sorry," Mary-Kate apologized. "I-I—" Her face grew pink.

I stepped in to save my sister. "Come on, Mary-Kate. We have to go get your eyes checked—remember?"

"When are we going to get our next clue?" Mary-Kate asked.

"I don't know. But I have an idea," I said. "Let's go hang with some real party animals."

Mary-Kate frowned. "What do you mean?" she asked.

"You'll see!" I grabbed her by the arm and led her to Disney's Animal Kingdom.

"*ROAR!*" Frightening sounds came out of Dinoland, USA.

"What is making those terrifying sounds?" Mary-Kate asked. "On second thought, I don't want to know."

I grabbed my sister's hand and led her to a seat on a big, open truck.

"Wow! Those dinosaurs look totally real," I said. "Look how their nostrils flare when they breathe!"

"That one's kind of cute," Mary-Kate said, pointing.

"But that one's definitely not!" I pointed at a dinosaur with horns like a bull, a toadlike face—and a really bad temper!

"For a minute there I thought we were dinosaur dinner," Mary-Kate said on the way out.

"I'm glad he wasn't the 'someone special' from the note!" I added.

"It's a jungle out there!" Mary-Kate cried. We were on the Kilimanjaro Safari, riding in the back of a big, open truck.

It was amazing to see so many wild African animals running free. We saw herds of zebras, hippopotamuses, lions, rhinoceroses, giraffes, and elephants.

"Whoa! Look how close that elephant is!" I cried. "I can almost reach out and touch it!"

"Hold on to your seats, folks!" our driver called. "I spotted some elephant hunters out there. We're going after them!"

The truck jerked forward, and we sped off over the rough ground.

I grabbed onto the seat in front of me. "Mary-Kate, do you think this is part of the tour?" I whispered.

Mary-Kate shrugged. "I don't know. But it's very cool!"

We chased the hunters over bridges, through valleys, and over hills. My heart pounded in my chest.

"Let's get 'em!" I cheered.

After our wild safari ride, we strolled over a bridge to a beautiful tropical island. A colorful village stood among the tropical plants and trees. The walls of all the buildings were carved and painted in bright colors.

I tapped Mary-Kate on the shoulder. "Mary-Kate, look over there!" I cried. "That's the biggest tree I have ever seen!"

It was called the Tree of Life. It was as tall as a fourteen-story building! And it looked just like a real tree—until you got up close.

"Wow! It has carvings of animals all over the trunk," Mary-Kate said. Eagles, snakes, bears, and other animals were carved into the bark of the tree.

"And it has a huge theater *inside* its trunk!" I added.

We took our seats in the theater. We put on 3-D glasses that looked like bug eyes. All kinds of bugs came flying at us!

"Aaah!" Mary-Kate cried.

She grabbed my arm when the show was over. "Don't mean to *bug* you," she said with a smile. "But let's go. We need to get our next clue!"

Our search for the clue led us to most magical place on Earth— the Magic Kingdom.

Suddenly my ears pricked up to the sound of familiar music. It was my favorite song. "That's 'When You Wish Upon A Star,'" I told Mary-Kate. "Can you hear it?"

Mary-Kate nodded. The sound of the music led us right to Cinderella's Golden Carousel.

"Oh, it's so beautiful!" Mary-Kate cried. "Let's take a ride. Pick a horse, Ashley."

It was hard to decide. Every horse was beautiful.

I ran over to a shimmering white stallion. "This is my horse," I said.

"But that's the one I just picked," Mary-Kate said.

We stared at each other. Then at the horse.

"Let's share," I suggested.

After our ride, I skipped away from the carousel, singing my favorite Disney songs.

"Get a grip, Ashley," Mary-Kate said.

I stared at my sister. "Excuse me?" I asked.

"Get a grip . . . on the sword," she said with a laugh. She pointed to a huge rock with a long dagger sticking out of it.

"The Sword in the Stone!" I cheered. "That's one of my favorite fairy tales!"

"And you know what they say," Mary-Kate added. "Whoever can pull the sword from the stone will rule the kingdom."

We grabbed the sword with both hands. Then we pulled and pulled with all our might.

"ARRRRRRGHHHH!" I grunted.

No matter how hard we tried, Mary-Kate and I could not wrestle that sword from the stone.

"Too bad we left Hercules back at MGM Studios," Mary-Kate said.

We left the Sword in the Stone and wandered through the Magic Kingdom.

"Oh, no!" Mary-Kate frowned. "What if the 'someone special' can't find us? Then we won't get our next clue!"

Just then we spotted two familiar figures in the distance.

"Mickey! Minnie!" Mary-Kate and I yelled together. Our favorite characters ran over to us and gave us big hugs.

"It's really you!" I exclaimed. "Minnie, you're even prettier in person."

"And you, too, Mickey," my sister added with a chuckle.

Mickey gave us a bashful look. Then he reached into his pocket and pulled out a piece of paper.

"He has a note for us!" I cried. "He's the 'someone special'!"

"We should have known," Mary-Kate said. "Who's more special than Mickey Mouse?"

We read the note carefully. It said:

COME TO TEA
THIS AFTERNOON
WE'D LOVE TO SEE YOU,
SO JOIN US SOON.
THE TEACUPS ARE
PUMPKIN ORANGE AND PINK
THEY'RE EASIER TO FIND
THAN YOU THINK.
YOU ARE SURE TO HAVE A BLAST,
BUT YOUR NEXT CLUE
WILL BE YOUR LAST.

*VROOOOM! VROOOOM!*

I turned to Mary-Kate. "What's that sound?"

We followed the roaring noise to a racetrack.

"Cool!" I called to Mary-Kate. "It's the Grand Prix Raceway. Let's go!"

We picked a bright-red race car.

"Okay," I said, rubbing my hands together. "Who's going to take this speed machine for a spin?"

Mary-Kate jumped into the driver's seat before I could say another word.

"But—" I started. "Okay, I'll drive after you." I jumped in beside her.

"Buckle up!" Mary-Kate announced. "It's going to be a bumpy ride!"

Then the car took off like a rocket. We screeched around the corners. We zoomed full speed down the straightaways.

It felt great to have the wind blowing through my hair as we sped down the track. But I was glad we weren't on a real freeway!

"So, what do you think?" Mary-Kate asked as we came to a screeching halt.

"I think I'm glad you don't have a real driver's license," I joked.

We quickly switched places, and I took my sister for a hair-raising spin.

"Time for tea?" Mary-Kate suggested.

We stood in front of a cluster of enormous pastel-colored teacups. It was an amazing sight.

"I guess we just found our tea party!" I said.

We picked one of the giant cups and piled in. Mary-Kate grabbed the wheel in the center and turned it. The teacup started spinning around and around.

"Not so fast, Mary-Kate," I begged.

A wicked smile spread across Mary-Kate's face. "No problem," she replied. Then she turned the wheel even faster!

"Whoa!" I cried. "I'm getting dizzy."

But Mary-Kate was having way too much fun.

Finally I felt the teacup slow down. Then it came to a stop. But my head didn't. It was still spinning!

I tumbled out of the teacup. "My legs feel like jelly." I had to pay Mary-Kate back. Big-time.

Mary-Kate grinned.
"That was the wildest tea
party I've ever been to!"

Suddenly someone tapped me on the shoulder. I turned around and saw Mickey.

"Hey, you're back!" I said. "What's up?"

Mickey handed Mary-Kate a note.

"Thanks!" she said. She started to read. But I grabbed her hand.

"Wait, Mary-Kate," I said. "This is our last note, remember? After this, our mystery will be solved. Then our Walt Disney World adventure might be over."

"Okay," she agreed. "We'll read it later." She tucked the note into her pocket.

"Do you hear singing?" I asked Mary-Kate.

She listened. "Yes! It's coming from over there." She pointed straight ahead of us.

"Let's check it out!" I suggested.

We took off toward the music. A sign outside a large building read IT'S A SMALL WORLD. We stepped inside and a pink boat floated toward us!

"Jump in!" Mary-Kate called.

We hopped into the boat and glided around a corner. Suddenly we were in a different world. Make that *many* different worlds! Hundreds of dolls from countries all around the world danced and sang in colorful costumes.

"Check out those cute wooden toy soldiers in England!" Mary-Kate cried.

Our boat took us round and round and round. "This place is huge!" I said as I stared at all the singing, dancing dolls.

"Maybe it should be called 'It's a Gigantic World!'" Mary-Kate joked.

"I don't want this day to end," I told Mary-Kate. "There's still so much to see!"

Mary-Kate's eyes lit up. "Like what?" she asked.

"Like Splash Mountain," I said. "Follow me!"

We raced across the Magic Kingdom to Splash Mountain.

"We'll sit up front," I suggested as we approached the ride. "I hear you don't get splashed there."

"Good," Mary-Kate said. "I just dried off from the Leapfrog Fountains."

"I know," I said, trying to hide a smile.

We piled into the first row of a giant log. We started our trip up the mountain.

"This is going to be great!" Mary-Kate beamed.

But she didn't know I was about to get my revenge for the teacup ride.

When we reached the top I turned to my sister and grinned. "Remember what I said about not getting wet if you sit up front?"

Suddenly we shot down a steep slope. We were headed straight for the water!

*SPLASSSSHHHH!*

"Gotcha!" I said triumphantly.

"Okay, you got me." Mary-Kate laughed as we climbed out of the log. "Should we read the note now?"

Before I could answer, Mary-Kate craned her neck to see something in the distance. "Ashley," she said. "I just saw Tommy and Jeffrey!"

"You mean our neighbors?" I asked. "Where?"

"Over by the Big Thunder Mountain Railroad. I'm going to say hi," she said.

"It's not them," I told my sister. "You're imagining it. Just like you imagined you saw Sarah and Jill. I won't let you go."

"How are you going to stop me?" Mary-Kate asked. "Lock me up?"

Hmmmm. Not a bad idea!

But even being locked up couldn't stop my sister from getting on the Big Thunder Mountain Railroad.

"It's a runaway train!" Mary-Kate cried as we sped through a flooded mining town.

"Look at the donkey swatting flies with his tail!" I shouted.

"Check out the man in the bathtub," Mary-Kate said. "He's floating down the main street!"

"I guess you were right about Tommy and Jeffrey," Mary-Kate admitted as we stepped out of the car. "I must be seeing things."

Finally I couldn't take the suspense any longer. "Let's read the note."

Mary-Kate took a deep breath. "Are you sure?" I nodded. Mary-Kate took out the note and read aloud:

YOU WANT TO KNOW
WHO BROUGHT YOU HERE
ALL THE ANSWERS
WILL SOON APPEAR.
READ THE RED WORDS
IN YOUR CLUES
PUT THEM TOGETHER
FOR THE NEWS.

LET GOOFY'S CLUE
LEAD THE WAY
TO THE BIGGEST SURPRISE
OF THE DAY.

I reached into my pocket and pulled out all the notes we had received that day. One by one I read the words in red out loud:

"Fairy godmother, a ball, coach, little mice, charming prince, pumpkin. And Goofy's clue was 'a castle with a tower high.'" Suddenly I knew the answer. "Mary-Kate, I think I know where we go next."

She grinned. "Me, too."

"Cinderella's Castle!" we shouted together.

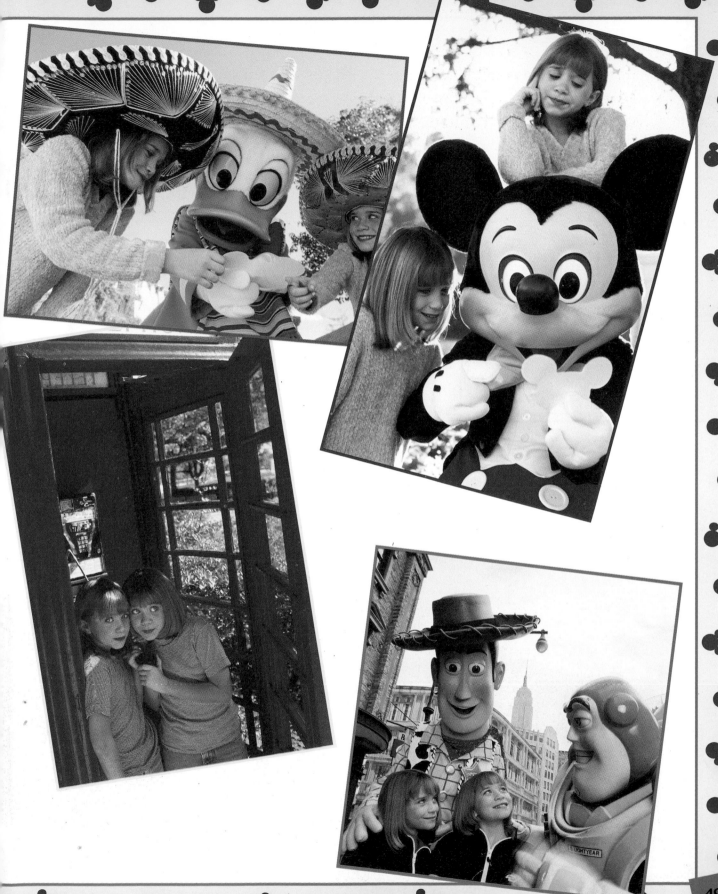

"It looks as if it's made out of diamonds!" I cried when we arrived at Cinderella's Castle. The huge towers seemed to float in the clouds.

"Look, the door's open," Mary-Kate said. "Let's go in."

I followed my sister down a long hallway. A lit room stood at the end.

When entered the room, it was empty.

"Maybe we were wrong about Cinderella's Ca—" I began.

"SURPRISE!" Suddenly a huge crowd of people jumped out from hiding places.

Mickey Mouse, Minnie Mouse, Donald, Buzz Lightyear, Woody, Hercules, Goofy, Pluto, Jasmine, Aladdin—they were all there!

"Mom! Dad! What are you doing here?" Mary-Kate cried when she spotted our parents in the crowd.

Then I saw our friends. "Jill. It *was* you!" I declared, giving my friend a squeeze.

"And Tommy and Jeffrey, too! And there's the real Sarah! What's going on here?"

"It's a surprise party for your birthday," my mother explained.

"But our birthday isn't until next month," Mary-Kate said.

"That's what makes it a surprise!" Our dad laughed.

We opened all of our presents, ate tons of birthday cake, and told everyone about our unbelievable day. Then Mary-Kate and I snuck outside for one last look at Walt Disney World.

"This was the best day of my whole life," I told my sister.

"Mine, too," Mary-Kate said. "I have an idea. Why don't we live here at Walt Disney World? Then we would never have to leave."

I laughed. "Don't worry, Mary-Kate," I
said. "We'll be back some day very soon."
Until then, we will keep the Disney
magic in our memories and in our hearts.

# Pick Up All-New Video Fun
## from MARY-KATE & ASHLEY

DUALSTAR VIDEO

# Listen To Us!

"Available Now on CD & Cassette"
Wherever Music Is Sold